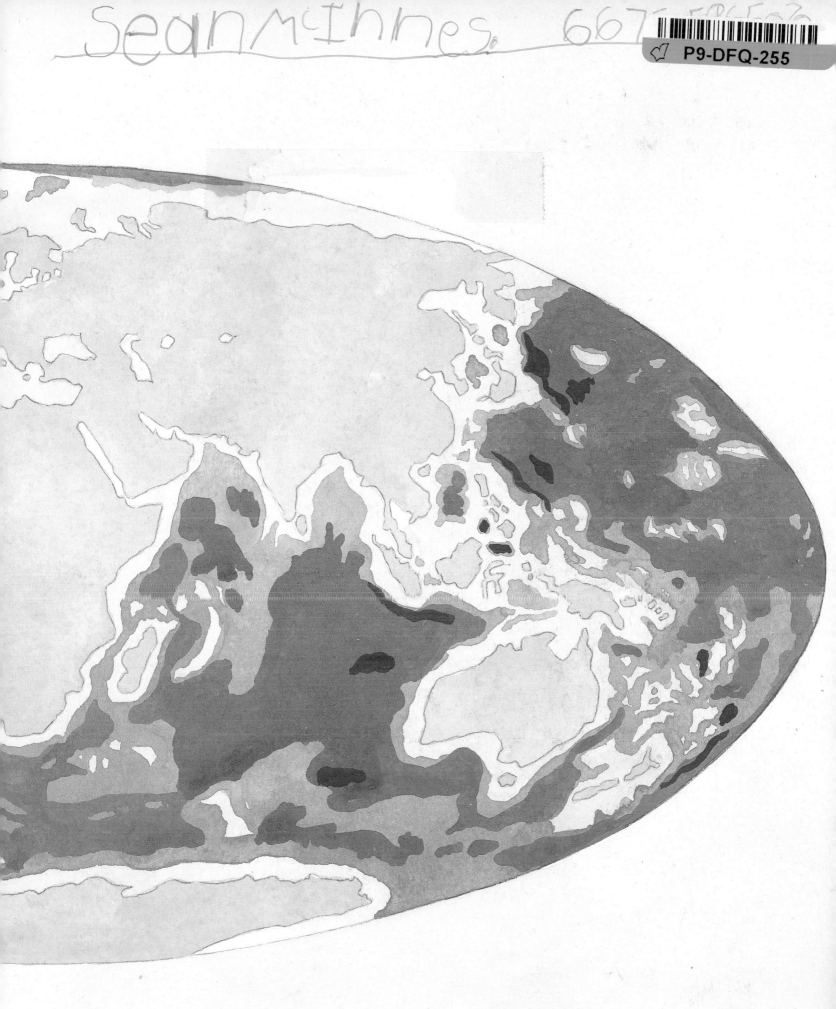

It should be noted that the illustrations have not been drawn to scale. Also, some of the creatures illustrated have been positioned in such a way to enable the reader to see them clearly. Naturally, some fish would be found at greater ocean depths than shown.

Edited by Belinda Gallagher
Cover design by Oxprint Ltd

ISBN 0 86112 749 8
© Brimax Books Ltd 1991. All rights reserved.
Published by Brimax Books Ltd, Newmarket, England 1991.
Printed in Portugal

UNDER THE OCEAN

Written by Judy Oglethorpe
Illustrated by Brian Watson

Contents

Brimax Books · Newmarket · England

The seas and oceans

We spend most of our time on land. Often we only see the sea at the beach and do not realise how big it is. In fact, about seven tenths of the Earth's surface is covered by sea, and only three tenths is land. Sea water tastes very salty to us. Over three quarters of the salt in sea water is sodium chloride, the salt which we use in cooking. There are also nitrates and other minerals in the water that are necessary for plant and animal life in the seas.

The map at the beginning of the book shows how deep the sea is. The lightest blue areas are less than 200 m (660 feet) deep. The name of each of these areas is the continental shelf and they occur where the land meets large oceans. From the continental shelf the seabed slopes down, sometimes quite steeply, to the plain of the ocean floor. As the shade of blue gets darker, the sea becomes deeper. Parts shown in dark blue are very deep – more than 6000 m below the surface of the sea (over three and a half miles). Some of these very deep areas are ocean trenches, deep splits in the plain of the ocean floor. The deepest point is in the Marianas Trench in the Pacific Ocean, approximately 11,000 m deep (nearly seven miles). This means it is deep enough to hold Mt Everest.

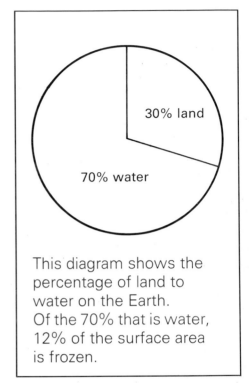

30% land

70% water

This diagram shows the percentage of land to water on the Earth.
Of the 70% that is water, 12% of the surface area is frozen.

Marianas Trench

Conditions at the bottom of the deep sea are very different to those on the surface. In very deep water there is no sunlight, so no plants can grow there, and there is much greater pressure because of the weight of water above. Also, deep sea water is cold. The temperature is always just above freezing point. This is very different to water at the sea's surface, which can be as cold as −2°C near the North and South Poles, and as warm as 35°C near the Equator. Creatures which live deep in the sea have adapted to the conditions there. They often lead a very different life to those animals which live in shallow waters.

Sea creatures which live on the shore have to be able to survive tides. The tide goes up and down twice a day. This leaves the creatures out of the water for part of the day.

If you have swum in the sea you may have noticed that there is often a current which tends to drag you along with it, sometimes out to sea and sometimes along the coast. There are many different currents in the oceans and they are very important to many sea creatures. Some use currents to help them on migration, from feeding grounds to breeding areas.

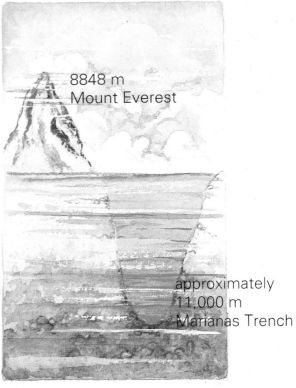

8848 m
Mount Everest

approximately
11,000 m
Marianas Trench

Continental Shelf

7

Creatures of the sea

Many different kinds of creatures live in the sea. Some can be seen at the beach: flounders, crabs, sea anemones, starfish and limpets. Bigger creatures, such as whales and tuna, live further out in the open sea. Some live in very deep water, such as the hatchet fish and angler fish.

The largest creature in the sea is the blue whale which can grow up to 29 m (97 feet) long. The smallest creatures are some of the plankton which can only be seen with a microscope. Plankton are made up of very small animals and plants, and the eggs and young of some larger creatures, and drift about in the sea water. Although plankton are small, they are very important as they are eaten by other bigger animals. The enormous blue whale eats animal plankton.

Some creatures are very bright, like corals and the fish that live amongst them. Others blend in with their surroundings so that they are less likely to be caught and eaten by other animals – this is called camouflage.

Key	
1	plankton
2	flounder
3	hermit crab
4	sea anemone
5	starfish
6	limpets
7	blue whale
8	tuna
9	angler fish
10	coral
11	seahorse
12	octopus
13	electric ray

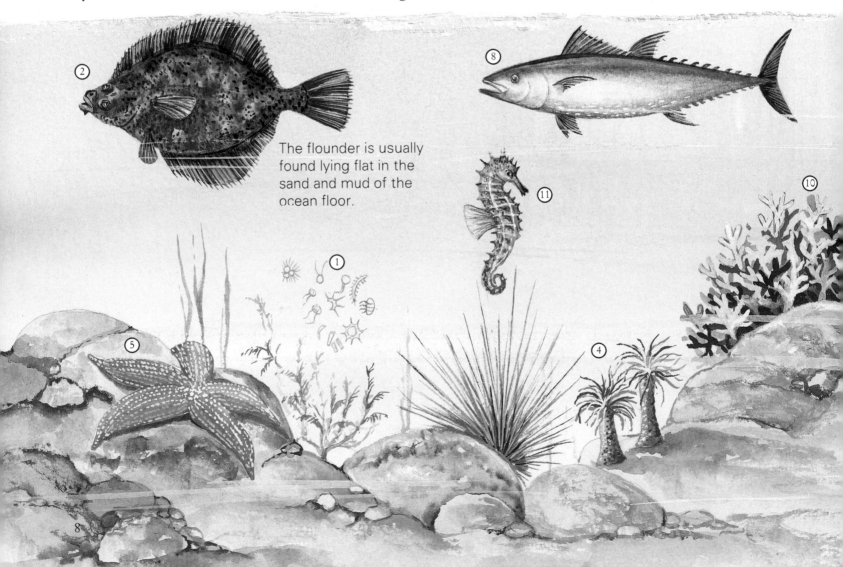

The flounder is usually found lying flat in the sand and mud of the ocean floor.

Many sea creatures look very strange, but there is always a reason for it. The little seahorse uses its long tail to hold onto seaweed to stop it being swept away by currents. The octopus uses its eight legs to walk on, and to catch animals to eat. The hermit crab lives inside a shell for protection from its enemies.

Some creatures have strange ways of catching their food. The angler fish has a long spine on its back. There is a little tuft on the tip which it uses as bait to attract other fish, which it eats. The electric ray produces powerful electric shocks to stun fish so that it can catch and eat them more easily.

We know quite a lot about sea creatures of shores and shallow waters as they are fairly easy to study. However, to find out about the creatures of the deep seas we have to use grabs or nets on the ends of very long cables, or remote-controlled underwater cameras. Recently, submersible vessels have been developed, which have a special chamber with air at atmospheric pressure and people can go down to very great depths in them. We are learning more about life in the deep seas all the time. There are probably still a lot of species of creatures which we have not yet discovered.

Who eats whom or what?

Like us, all sea creatures have to eat to survive. Different creatures have different ways of feeding, and feed on different kinds of food. In the Antarctic Ocean, plant plankton are eaten by krill, a kind of animal plankton. Krill are eaten by squid. Seals eat squid. Killer whales eat seals. This process is called a food chain.

plant plankton

krill

squid

seal

killer whale

Food chains always start with plants. The most common plants in the sea are the tiny plant plankton which drift in open water. Although they are small there are so many of them that they are at the start of most food chains in the sea. Other plants grow in coastal waters. Seaweeds and green plants called algae grow on rocks. Coral reefs have very special plants. Corals are animals, but most of them have tiny plants living inside their bodies.

All these plants in the sea use sunlight, water and a substance called carbon dioxide to make sugars. They also take nitrate and phosphate salts from the sea water, and they use all these substances to grow.

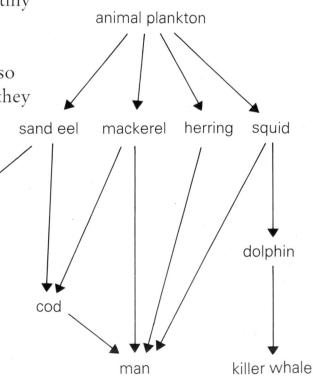

plant plankton

animal plankton

sand eel   mackerel   herring   squid

puffin

cod

dolphin

black-backed gull

man

killer whale

The next step is when an animal eats a plant and uses the plant material for its own growth. Limpets feed on seaweed and green algae on the rocks. Parrot fish and surgeon fish eat coral, and therefore the tiny plants growing inside it. Many kinds of animal plankton feed on plant plankton.

surgeon fish

coral

parrot fish

limpets

At the next step in the food chain, animals which feed on plants are eaten by other animals. Animal plankton are important food for many creatures. Included in animal plankton are the young stages of many kinds of fish, as well as starfish, jellyfish, worms, crabs, and also the eggs of some fish. They are eaten by many different kinds of fish and by some seabirds, squid, and even some kinds of shark and whale.

Finally, we get to the top of the food chain – to an animal which is not normally caught and eaten by any other. We ourselves are at the top of many food chains in the sea, as we eat many sea creatures.

Some animals do not only feed on living things – they also eat dead plants and animals, or their remains. Crabs, prawns and some sea urchins eat parts of dead animals. Lugworms eat small bits of dead material in the sand and mud. The substances in the dead animals and plants are therefore recycled to living creatures.

This food chain begins with the simplest of plant plankton which supports bigger, more complex forms of life until reaching the most powerful animal of all – man.

How do sea creatures move?

Nearly all sea creatures have to move to catch or find food. Many also move to escape from predators. Some travel long distances to breed and feed. There are very many different ways of moving in the sea.

Tuna fish, penguins and dolphins are very different types of animal (fish, bird and mammal), but they all have the same sort of shape when swimming. They have smooth, streamlined outlines, with no parts sticking out to drag against the water they are moving through.

Most swimming animals use their tails to drive them through the water, or webbed feet in the case of birds, and hind flippers in seals. They steer by using their other fins, wings or flippers.

However, skates and rays have large, wing-like fins which they flap to move. Sea lions use their front flippers for propulsion and steer with their hind flippers. Turtles use all four limbs like paddles.

Key

1 sea lion
2 penguin
3 tuna
4 shark
5 dolphin
6 octopus
7 turtle
8 manta
9 ray
10 flying fish

The fastest speed recorded for a swimming animal is for a sailfish – nearly 110 km per hour (68 mph). Dolphins are the fastest mammals and have been recorded at 56 km per hour (35 mph). Some penguins can swim at up to 32 km per hour (20 mph). They use their wings as well as their webbed feet for propulsion. Some of the fastest animals, like sailfish, tunas, dolphins and whales, can even leap out of the water. When flying fish are being chased by predators, they can launch themselves out of the water and spread their side fins like wings, gliding for several metres.

Swimming is not the only way to move. Lobsters and crabs usually crawl about on the sea bottom, using their long legs. Only when in danger do they swim away backwards to hide. The octopus moves around slowly on its eight long tentacles. In an emergency it shoots a jet of water backwards from its body and moves away very fast. Sea snails glide over rocks and weeds using their muscular 'foot'. Starfish and sea urchins have thousands of tiny suckers in rows on their hard shells, which allow the animal to glide slowly in any direction.

Although plankton drift in currents, some animal plankton can also move under their own power. Some have legs, cilia (hair-like projections which twist to make them move), or tentacles for swimming with.

Rocky shores

Many different kinds of creatures live on rocky shores. Each species lives in slightly different conditions from the rest. Often, a particular species only occurs at a certain level on the rocks. Mussels are found between the low and high tide levels and are covered in sea water and then exposed to the air twice a day. They open their paired shells to filter feed when the tide is up, and close them when it goes down to stop themselves from drying out. The barnacles are usually higher up on the rock, and therefore can spend less time feeding.

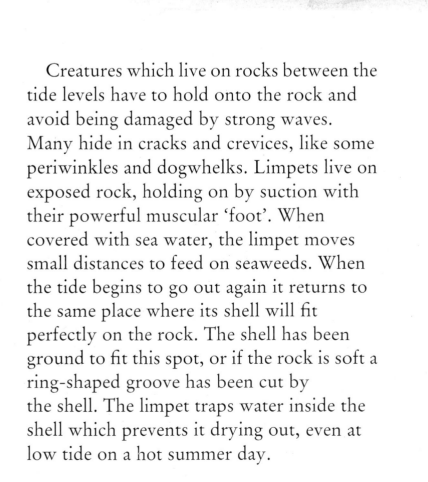

Creatures which live on rocks between the tide levels have to hold onto the rock and avoid being damaged by strong waves. Many hide in cracks and crevices, like some periwinkles and dogwhelks. Limpets live on exposed rock, holding on by suction with their powerful muscular 'foot'. When covered with sea water, the limpet moves small distances to feed on seaweeds. When the tide begins to go out again it returns to the same place where its shell will fit perfectly on the rock. The shell has been ground to fit this spot, or if the rock is soft a ring-shaped groove has been cut by the shell. The limpet traps water inside the shell which prevents it drying out, even at low tide on a hot summer day.

Grey sea slugs eat sea anemones. They are not affected by the anemones' stinging tentacles. The slug cannot move fast but it has a growth on its back that looks similar to the anemone's tentacles. This may confuse predators.

Dogwhelks eat creatures with shells, such as barnacles, limpets, periwinkles and mussels. It can bore a narrow hole through the shell of its prey with its horny 'tongue'. Once through, it scrapes out the soft inside parts. This can take the dogwhelk two days, but if the prey has two shells like the mussel, it may be able to force them apart and feed more quickly.

Key
1 sea slug
2 sea anemone
3 dogwhelk
4 barnacles
5 mussel

A very unusual creature living on rocky shores of the Galapagos Islands is the marine iguana. It is the only lizard which swims in the sea. Between dives it basks in the sun on the rocks. It can grow up to 1.5 m (5 feet) long, and feeds on seaweeds.

15

Sandy and muddy shores

When the tide is out, very few creatures can be seen living on the sand. There are creatures there, but most of them are in burrows below the surface, or hiding in pieces of seaweed washed up at the high tide mark. During the day beach fleas live in shallow burrows near the high tide line. They hop down to the water's edge at night to feed on plankton. In some places ghost crabs hunt for the remains of dead animals amongst the weed. When they are not moving they are difficult to see as they are the same colour as the sand. When in danger they scuttle into the sea for safety.

Lower down the beach some animals live in the sand. Cockles and razors use their muscular 'foot' to dig themselves in. When the tide comes in razors use their siphons to obtain food above the sand. Cockles take in water and filter out their food from it.

Different kinds of creatures live lower down the beach where the sand is nearly always covered with water. Sea potatoes and some sea cucumbers burrow in the sand, eating small particles of dead material. The sea potato is a kind of sea urchin. The sand mason worm builds a tube to live in. The tube is lined with a sticky substance produced by the worm's skin. At high tide the sandmason climbs up its tube and its tentacles sweep over the sand surface for small particles of food. The lugworm lives in

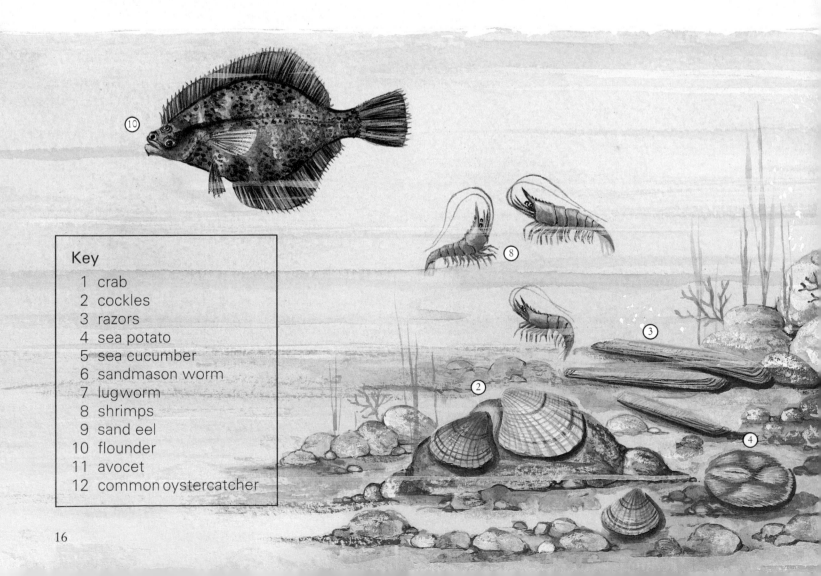

Key
1 crab
2 cockles
3 razors
4 sea potato
5 sea cucumber
6 sandmason worm
7 lugworm
8 shrimps
9 sand eel
10 flounder
11 avocet
12 common oystercatcher

a burrow and eats sand which falls into it from the surface. The lugworm feeds on tiny animals and dead material in the sand. The remaining sand it has eaten is deposited on the surface in the familiar coiled wormcasts.

Some shrimps hide just below the surface of the sand during the day, coming out at night to feed. In the shallow water above the sand there may be sand-eels and flounders; they can also bury themselves in the sand.

Muddy shores often have many more different kinds of creatures than sandy shores, especially if the mud is firm. The mud is richer in food than sand as more dead material is deposited, and this supports a large number of creatures. Eel grass may grow here, with some kinds of shrimps and prawns living amongst the plants.

Many different species of birds feed on sandy and muddy shores. Their long legs allow them to wade in shallow water. Bills of different species vary in shape and size, so many different kinds of birds can feed together in the same area without competing directly with each other.

Coral reefs

Corals and the creatures which live around them are some of the most beautiful animals in the sea. Coral reefs only occur in warm, clear, shallow waters. Corals need warm water to grow in, and sunlight to reach the tiny plants living inside the corals. The coral animal has tentacles, which open at night and capture plankton.

Corals live in colonies – millions of corals grow close together. Each small coral animal builds a hard, chalky skeleton around itself. The skeletons join together, forming coral heads which sometimes have fantastic shapes. As older corals die, young corals grow on their skeletons, and so the coral reef develops. Coral grows particularly fast where there is a good current rich in plankton. Sometimes reefs are very large. The most famous is the Great Barrier Reef off the coast of Australia.

In coral reefs, there are many corridors, holes, mazes and crags, so there are very many places for other creatures to live. Small butterfly fish stay near to the reef, hiding in crevices when in danger. Some butterfly fish have long snouts for probing into cracks to find worms and other small animals. Moray eels lurk in deep crevices in the coral. They do not have protective scales on their body, so they hide from predators. But as other fish swim past they grab them with their dog-like jaws and sharp teeth, and eat them whole.

Key
1 butterfly fish
2 moray eel
3 clown fish
4 parrot fish
5 puffer fish
6 sea anemone

sea fan   sea feather   brain coral   stag's horn

Clown fish have another kind of protection – they live near large sea anemones, but are protected from their stings by a layer of slime covering their skin. When in danger they can hide among the anemones' tentacles. In return the anemones probably get scraps from the clown fishes' meals, and are cleaned by them. Parrot fish also use a layer of slime for protection against other fish, when they sleep in a hole in the coral at night. During the day they feed on corals. Puffer fish, which also feed on corals, blow themselves up like a balloon when alarmed, to make themselves look bigger.

Many of the coral reef fish have bright markings because they have a small area on the reef where they live on their own or with a mate. This area is the 'territory'. If another fish of the same species comes into the area, the occupant will try to chase it away. The bright markings let the other fish recognise it and warn it that the area is already occupied. Other creatures besides fish live on coral reefs, including crabs, sea urchins, sponges, sea squirts, clams and tube-building worms.

On the Great Barrier Reef, the crown-of-thorns starfish feeds on the living parts of the coral. Recently it has become much more common, perhaps because people have over-collected the beautiful triton snails which eat the starfish. The starfish are now destroying large areas of coral.

Other creatures of coastal waters

Creatures of coastal waters live on the seabed, float on the surface, or live in the water in between.

Jellyfish come in many different colours. Some float on the surface of the sea and some kinds swim in deeper water, as well as the open sea. Their bodies consist mostly of water.

Many are umbrella-shaped on top with tentacles dangling below, surrounding the mouth. Many jellyfish feed on animals such as shrimps and small fish. Stings on the tentacles paralyse these animals, which are then transferred to the mouth by the tentacles. The stings of some jellyfish can be harmful to man. However, a few creatures manage to avoid being harmed by the stings. Young whiting often collect beneath pink jellyfish, inside the curtain of tentacles. This protects them from their enemies until they are big enough to swim in the shoals of adult whiting.

The cone shell is another animal which catches its food by paralysing it. Cone shells are sea snails which live on the seabed in warm, shallow waters. They have beautiful, cone-shaped shells. They are mostly active at night, feeding on worms, and even fish. They have poisonous teeth on the end of a long tube, which they thrust into their prey's body. It is paralysed in seconds, and is then eaten at leisure. Some cone shells can give a painful sting to man, and a few can even kill.

Sponges are animals which grow on rocks or corals. Each sponge consists of a supporting meshwork surrounding many little openings through which it draws water. Food is obtained from the water – mostly tiny bits of dead plants and animals. Bath sponges grow in warm seas, mostly in the eastern Mediterranean and the seas off Florida and the Bahamas.

Cuttlefish live in coastal waters. They are related to the squid and octopus, and like them have tentacles. They normally swim using a fin round the edge of the body, but can also move very fast by shooting out a jet of water. They send jets of water on the sand of the seabed to uncover animals such as shrimps which they eat.

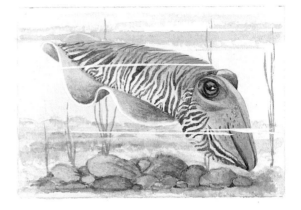

Coastal waters are important areas for many fish. Some live there all their lives. Others like the herring travel there each year from deeper waters to lay their eggs. A most unusual fish which lives on the seabed of coastal waters in parts of the Indian Ocean was only discovered in 1938. It is a living fossil – the coelacanth. It is quite unlike other fishes, having different kind of scales and short limbs with fins on. It is the only known living survivor of a group of fishes called lobe-fins which were common 300 million years ago.

coelacanth

Mammals of the sea

Whales, dolphins and porpoises have fish-like body shapes, but they are not fish. They are mammals – animals with warm blood, that breathe air and suckle their young. Several types of mammal live in the sea.

Some sea mammals do not spend all of their time in the sea but come out on land to breed and sometimes to sleep and bask in the sun. Seals, sealions, and walruses breed in colonies on land or ice, and most individuals return to the same breeding grounds each year. The males of some species have their own territories and will fight off other males which approach, to protect their female mates. The pups grow very quickly, as their mothers' milk is very rich. After the breeding season all the animals return to the sea to feed and may travel far from the coast. Nearly all species stay in cold waters.

Walruses occur only in the Arctic. They have long tusks which may be more than 1 m (3 feet) long in adult males. They use the tusks to rake up shellfish at the bottom of the sea for food, and for defence against killer whales and polar bears. They also use them to get a grip on ice or stone when they are starting to haul themselves out of the water.

Sea otters live along the shores of the northern Pacific Ocean. They have a thick layer of fur to keep them warm. They live in small groups among beds of seaweed and feed on fish and shellfish. To open shellfish a sea otter floats on its back in the water and balances a stone on its stomach, smashing the shellfish against it.

Some sea mammals stay in water all the time and never come out on land. The sea cows – manatees and dugongs – live in tropical coastal waters, and some species also move into rivers and estuaries at times. They feed entirely on sea grasses and other water plants.

Whales, dolphins and porpoises also stay in the sea all the time. They are found in all oceans of the world. Some live in shallow coastal waters while others live in the open seas. Dolphins and porpoises are related to whales but are smaller. They eat mostly fish and squid.

Dolphins are very intelligent creatures, and are able to learn and copy many actions when they come into contact with man. They mostly live in groups, sometimes numbering several thousand. Bottlenose dolphins work closely with other members of the group. When a female is giving birth, two other adult females wait nearby for the baby to emerge, tail first. They then move in together and guide it up to the surface for its first breath.

sea otter

manatee

common dolphin

Whales

There are two main kinds of whales, toothed whales and baleen whales. Baleen whales are mostly larger, and include the blue whale which can grow as long as 29 m (97 feet). This is the largest living creature on Earth.

The two kinds of whales feed in very different ways. Toothed whales have teeth and feed on other animals such as fish, squid and cuttlefish.

Baleen whales have whalebone, called baleen, in their mouths. This consists of horny plates which hang down from the upper jaw to form a sieve. The whale feeds by taking in mouthfuls of water and pushing the water out through the whalebone with its tongue. Plankton and other small animals in the water are trapped and swallowed. Baleen whales have enormous mouths to enable them to get enough food.

Whales, like dolphins and porpoises, breathe air through a blowhole on the highest point of the head above the snout. Some whales can stay underwater for an hour and a half before they need to go to the surface to breathe again. As they breathe out they produce a spout. Whales can often be identified by the shape of the spout.

blue whale

minke whale

humpback whale

bowhead whale

great right whale and calf

Whales are warm-blooded and have to keep warm. They have a thick layer of fat called blubber under their skins to insulate them. The blubber is especially thick in whales which live in cold waters. Two fifths of the great right whale's body weight is blubber.

Whale calves suckle from their mothers underwater. The milk contains much fat and they grow very quickly. Mothers take great care of their young, keeping constant watch over them.

Most species of whales are sociable creatures and live in groups called pods. Both young and adults spend time playing. Also, if one whale becomes sick or injured the others may support it from below and raise it to the water surface so that it can breathe.

Whales communicate with each other by making sounds. We can hear some of these sounds with our ears but others are outside our range of hearing so we cannot listen to them without special equipment. The sounds make up complicated 'songs' with different meanings. We know that some whale sounds can travel a great distance in the ocean: for example, fin whale sounds can travel over 800 km (500 miles).

Toothed whales also use sound to help them navigate, by a system called echolocation, as bats do. They can detect sounds they have made when they bounce back off rocks and other objects. They are able to work out where the objects are and avoid bumping into them. This is very useful in deep or murky water where it is difficult to see.

Other members of the pod will help a sick or injured whale.

Sharks and rays

Sharks and rays are fish. Sharks occur in all oceans, especially in the tropics. There are many different kinds of shark. Sharks' bodies are heavier than water and would sink if they were still, so those which live in the open seas must swim all the time.

Many sharks have a very good sense of smell. They can detect blood in the water from a few hundred metres away. When a shark picks up a smell it moves in zig-zags trying to find the direction the smell is coming from.

Some sharks have large, razor-sharp teeth and often attack anything which moves and seems edible. Occasionally they attack people, although only in warm waters. One of the most dangerous sharks to man is the white shark, which can grow to 5 m (16 feet) in length.

Occasionally, sharks have hitch-hikers. The remora has a sucker on its back. It uses the sucker to stick to the shark without damaging it. The remora gains protection and transport, and may feed on scraps from the shark's meals. It probably also eats parasites on the shark's body, so the shark benefits from its hitch-hiker.

Eagle rays and mantas also live in the open sea. The manta can grow to more than 6 m (19 feet) in length and weigh one and a half tons. But it feeds on plankton, swimming with its mouth open and funnelling the food into 'horns' at the side of the mouth.

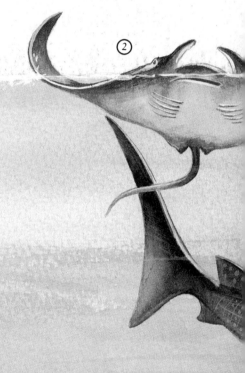

Sharks have a reputation for attacking people, but this is true only of some species. The large basking shark is harmless as it has no teeth and feeds on plankton, small fish and squid. It swims along with its huge mouth wide open. Water enters and passes through the gills. The food is sieved out by rakers (sieves) along the gills.

Many other rays live on the sea bed, and some bury themselves in the sand to hide from predators. The sting-ray has a backward-pointing spine on the middle of its tail which is connected with a poison gland. The stings can be very painful and harmful to man. The electric ray can produce powerful electric shocks, both to protect it from predators and to stun fish so that it can catch and eat them more easily.

Sharks and rays have some other unusual features. On the snout they have small pits which can detect an extra sense – the Earth's magnetic field. They can use this to work out direction.

Key
1 white shark
2 manta
3 sting ray
4 electric ray
5 whale shark
6 hammerhead shark
7 basking shark

Other fish of the open sea

Many other kinds of fish live in the open seas. Most of them are found quite near the surface, as most food occurs there. Plant plankton live only in the top 100 m (330 feet) or so of water where there is enough sunlight for them to grow, and most food chains in the open seas start with plant plankton.

Many types of fish live in shoals, sometimes with several thousands of fish of the same species staying together – herring, mackerel and anchovies do this. As they swim, each fish in the shoal changes direction at exactly the same time. If a predator approaches, they bunch up together for protection. In this way, the chance of any one fish being captured and eaten is very small.

Herring are dark-coloured on the top of the body and silvery underneath. When seen from above they blend with the darkness beneath them, and when seen from the side or below their silvery flanks reflect the light of the water around them. This makes it difficult for predators to see them clearly.

Other fish of the open seas include tuna, albacore, swordfish and sailfish. They are related to the mackerel but are much larger. They are all predators which eat other fish, and live mostly in the top 200 m (660 feet) of water.

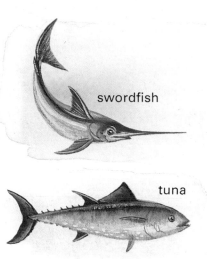

swordfish

tuna

There is one large area of open sea where fish can find shelter from predators. In the Sargasso Sea, east of the southern United States, large quantities of Sargassum weed drift in circular currents on the surface. The little Sargassum fish is the same colour as the weed and its body is covered with weed-like growths, including false air bladders. The pipe fish's long, thin body looks like a stem of weed.

Sargassum fish

Although most fish occur in the top 200 m of the sea, some are found in deeper waters. One is the small hatchet fish, so-called because of its hatchet-like shape. It is found between 100 and 500 m where there is very dim sunlight. The hatchet fish has very large eyes, probably to make most use of the blue-green light there.

hatchet fish

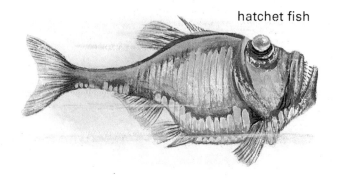

When we are in the sea, unless we are actively swimming or making ourselves float we tend to sink because our bodies are heavier than water. However, many fish (apart from sharks) are able to remain motionless at various depths in the sea without sinking. This is because they have a chamber inside their bodies called a swim bladder which contains gas. It keeps them buoyant. Fish can alter the amount of gas in the swim bladder depending on the depth of water they are in.

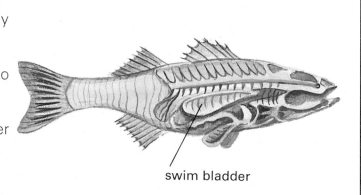

swim bladder

Creatures of the deep

In the very deep oceans there is no sunlight, and no plants grow. The creatures here eat other creatures or dead material, most of which comes from above.

Sea cucumbers plough their way through the ooze of fine mud and dead matter on the seabed, swallowing it and obtaining food from it. Other creatures such as some starfish and brittle stars pick out particles of dead material.

Many animals living on the seabed have long stalks or legs to stay well clear of the ooze. Some sea spiders have legs 60 cm (2 feet) long. The feathery-looking sea pens have long stalks. Despite the great pressures at these depths many of the creatures are graceful and slender-looking. They do not need strong shells or skeletons as there are no tides and currents to buffet them.

There are fewer creatures living in deep seas because there is less food. There may be a long wait between meals. Many creatures have developed enormous mouths, powerful jaws and expanding stomachs to catch and swallow a wide range of

Key	
1	sea cucumber
2	starfish
3	brittle star
4	sea spider
5	sea pens
6	gulper eel
7	deep sea angler fish
8	hatchet fish
9	lantern fish
10	football fish
11	squid
12	ray

prey including quite large creatures. The gulper eel can even swallow fish larger than itself. Its stomach expands like a balloon, collapsing again as it digests its meal.

Many of the fish have very small eyes or even no eyes at all, since there is no sunlight. However, some of the creatures produce light themselves. They do this by making a substance called luciferin. Many creatures produce this light – including animals living in shallower waters. Some animals glow, but most produce flashes of light. Sea pens light up when touched. We are not sure what all the purposes of this luminescence are: perhaps to recognise mates, or confuse enemies when being attacked. Poisonous creatures may use it to warn predators to leave them alone. Some deep-sea angler fish have a luminescent lure, drawing little fish to the light.

As there are fewer creatures in the ocean depths, it is more difficult for males and females to meet to breed. The deep sea angler fish has found a way round this – the male is much smaller than the female, so when they meet he fuses to her body. He is carried around by her and they can breed several times.

deep sea angler fish

31

Sea creatures which migrate

Not all sea creatures live in the same place all the year round or for all of their lives. Some of them travel very long distances, to feed or to breed.

Some species of baleen whales migrate long distances. They feed in the cold, plankton-rich waters near the Arctic and Antarctic during the summer, and in the winter when the icepack closes in they move towards the Equator into warm, tropical waters where they calve.

The smallest creatures also migrate. Plankton may travel long distances on ocean currents. In cold seas, animal plankton migrate vertically. They spend the summer near the surface when there is a good food supply, and the winter down in the depths.

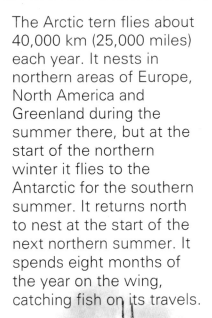

The Arctic tern flies about 40,000 km (25,000 miles) each year. It nests in northern areas of Europe, North America and Greenland during the summer there, but at the start of the northern winter it flies to the Antarctic for the southern summer. It returns north to nest at the start of the next northern summer. It spends eight months of the year on the wing, catching fish on its travels.

Key

1 Arctic tern
2 European eel
3 humpback whale
4 green turtle
5 grey whale

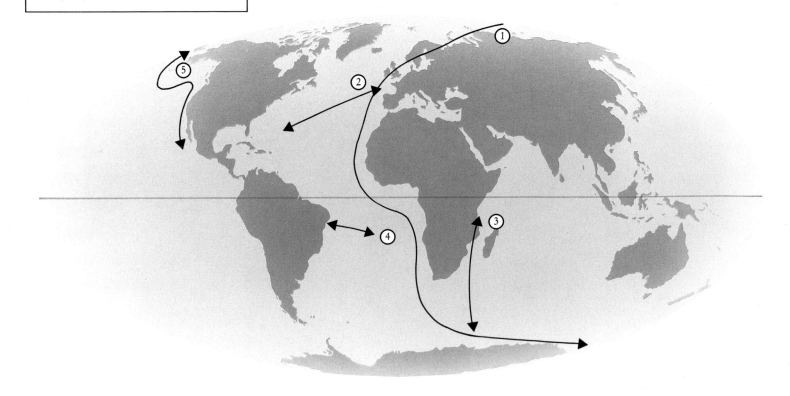

Some fish live part of their lives in the sea and part in fresh water. Young European eels hatch in the Sargasso Sea. They are carried by the Gulf Stream to European coasts, arriving when they are two or three years old. They swim up rivers, and can even travel short distances overland to land-locked ponds.

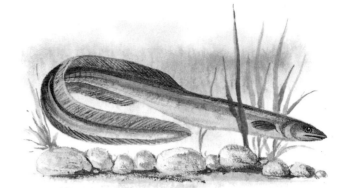

Salmon breed in freshwater streams, and the young spend a few years in fresh water before swimming downstream to the sea. They feed and grow in the sea before returning to rivers to breed. Amazingly, they return to the same stream where they were hatched, probably recognising the smell or taste of the water.

Sea turtles migrate large distances across the oceans between their feeding and breeding grounds. The female green turtle lays her eggs on tropical sandy beaches above the high tide mark. When the eggs hatch the young turtles must rush towards the sea, often past hordes of predators.

Some green turtles lay eggs on Ascension Island in the Atlantic Ocean. They then travel to the coast of Brazil to feed. This is about 2250 km (1400 miles) away. How they find their way back to Ascension, a tiny island only 8 km (5 miles) wide in the middle of the Atlantic, is a mystery.

Birds of the sea

There are very many different kinds of sea bird. Some, like gulls and cormorants, live around the coast and feed in shallow waters. Others spend most of the year at sea, feeding far from land. They only return to land to breed. Examples are albatrosses, petrels and shearwaters.

The largest of all the sea birds is the wandering albatross which has a wingspan of more than 3 m (10 feet). It lives in the southern oceans and feeds on squid, fish and krill. Young albatrosses spend several years at sea before landing on a remote island to join a breeding colony. It takes several months for a fledgling to leave its parents, so a pair breeds once every two years, producing one offspring at a time. Albatrosses pair for life and can live for 80 years.

Many sea birds nest in colonies. Often hundreds of pairs of one species nest very close to each other on small islands or cliffs. This gives more protection against predators. One species which nests in colonies is the gannet. The adult gannets fly out to sea to catch fish for themselves and their young.

albatross

Most sea birds find or catch their own food, but the skua is also a pirate. It chases other birds such as terns and forces them to drop their last catch. The skua then eats the stolen food.

Sea birds are well adapted to their way of life. Nearly all have webbed feet to help them to swim. They produce an oily

gannet

tern

skua

substance which is spread over the feathers during preening. This waterproofs them. They also have a thick layer of soft down feathers under the outer ones to keep warm. Air trapped in the feathers helps them to float.

Penguins spend a lot of time swimming and diving, but do not float like other sea birds. They have small, closely packed feathers which makes them less buoyant. A thick layer of blubber beneath the skin keeps them warm. Penguins cannot fly. Their wings are small and are used for swimming. All penguins live in cold waters, in the southern hemisphere except for the Galapagos penguin. It lives on the Equator, on the Galapagos Islands where there is a cold current of water from the Antarctic.

emperor penguin

Galapagos penguins

Some other birds have wings which are better adapted for swimming than for flying – for example, puffins, razorbills and guillemots. Puffins nest on soft grassy slopes, in burrows which they line with grass, feathers or sea plants.

puffins

Why are sea creatures important to us?

For many thousands of years man has been making use of sea creatures. Shellfish were collected by prehistoric man – we know this because of the shells found near his dwelling sites. More recently, man developed hooks and nets to catch fish. When man invented rafts and boats he ventured out to sea and started to catch a wider range of sea creatures.

With modern boats and equipment we now use sea creatures more than ever before. Each year we catch millions of tons of fish, including tuna, pilchard, sardine, anchovy, cod, haddock, mackerel and herring. We also catch squid, and shellfish such as shrimps, prawns, crabs, lobsters, mussels and oysters. Much of the catch is eaten by people – fresh, frozen, tinned, smoked, salted or dried. A large quantity is also ground up to make fishmeal for some farm animals.

Besides fishing, we also farm sea creatures in many parts of the world. These include salmon, plaice, milkfish, oysters, mussels and clams. This can be very productive, so farming is likely to increase in future years.

For many centuries man has hunted whales. The whaling industry began in the tenth century AD when the North Atlantic right whale was hunted. Up to the mid-nineteenth century, oil was made from blubber and used for lighting. Baleen was used for sieves, corsets and carriage springs. Meat was eaten. More recently many other whale products were developed. Margarine, soap, candles, crayons, cosmetics, industrial oil, pet food, livestock feeds and fertilisers were all made from parts of whales.

Dolphins, porpoises and seals have also been killed for their meat and oil, and furs are obtained from fur seals. Green turtles are edible and are used to make turtle soup. Shells of hawksbill turtles are used for tortoise-shell. Turtle eggs are also eaten.

Shells have been used for thousands of years by man. Cowries were used in many parts of the world as money. Caribbean conch shells were used as trumpets. Pearl oyster shells have a lining of mother-of-pearl, and this is used in jewellery. Pearls come from pearl oysters in the tropical areas of the Pacific and Indian Oceans. The red coral which grows in the Mediterranean region, has been collected for a long time for ornaments, charms and medicine.

We use sea creatures for other purposes, too. Medicinal drugs are being developed from some animals. Some kinds of tropical sponges are harvested, though most bath sponges are now made of plastic.

conch shell

Over-harvesting and its effects

When whaling began, only the slower swimming whales could be caught by men hunting from rowing boats with harpoons and spears. These were right, bowhead and grey whales. By the beginning of the twentieth century they had been over-hunted and were scarce. By then whalers had more powerful boats and harpoon guns, so they turned to the faster fin, humpback and blue whales. The humpback and blue whales were becoming scarce by the 1950s and 1960s so fin, sperm and sei whales then became the main catch. In the early 1960s over 90,000 whales were slaughtered in one year. There were fewer and fewer whales left with each year of whaling.

Whales breed slowly, therefore whale numbers dropped because many more whales were being killed than were being born. People in many countries feared that some species of whale would disappear completely – in other words, become extinct. The hunting of the badly affected species was banned. Most countries stopped whaling in the 1960s and 1970s to let the populations recover. By 1988 only Japan, Norway and Iceland were still whaling, killing a relatively small number for research.

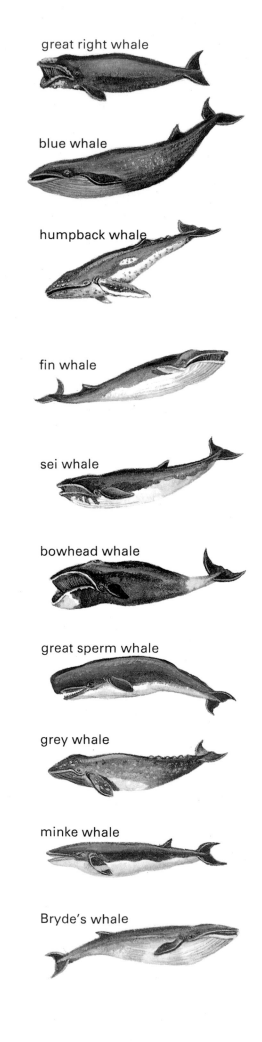

great right whale

blue whale

humpback whale

fin whale

sei whale

bowhead whale

great sperm whale

grey whale

minke whale

Bryde's whale

Data from the International Whaling Commission

SPECIES	ORIGINAL POPULATION	PRESENT POPULATION (1988)
sperm whale	2,400 000	2,000 000
right whales	100 000+	3 500
bowhead whale	30 000+	7 500
grey whale	20 000+	19 000
fin whale	500 000+	120 000
humpback whale	115 000	10 000
blue whale	230 000	15 000
sei whale	170 000	40 000
minke whale	600 000	600 000
Bryde's whale	90 000	90 000

Numbers of grey whales and some right whales have since increased, but we do not know yet whether the others will recover.

In the North Sea, herring and mackerel were over-fished in the 1960s and their numbers fell. Some fishermen turned to catching capelin, and others to catching sprats. This completely changed the composition of the North Sea catch. It now contains many more small fish like sprats and sand eels.

Fishing can cause direct damage to other animals. Dolphins feed on yellowfin tuna in the eastern Pacific and hundreds of thousands of dolphins were drowned every year in fishermen's nets. Many fishermen now try to save the dolphins, because people in other parts of the world were so worried about the dolphins they stopped buying the tuna.

Sea creatures have been overhunted until some are at risk of becoming extinct. We have gained food or other products for a short while, but it has proved to be wasteful and irresponsible in the long term. It would be much better to fish a population carefully, not taking any more than the creatures can replace through breeding each year. This way it is possible to fish that population for many years. This is called sustained use.

One of the main problems is that nobody owns the sea, and it is difficult to get different countries to agree about how many fish or whales each can take. Properly managed, the sea would be a valuable source of food for millions of people for many years.

herring

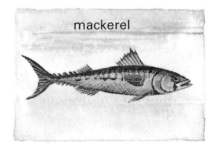

mackerel

capelin

sprats and sand eels

Pollution of the seas

We dump much of our wastes in the sea. Until quite recently, not much thought was given to what happened to them. It seemed that the sea was big enough to take everything. We now dump very large amounts of many different substances and it is clear they are causing harm to sea plants and creatures and sometimes to ourselves. This is called pollution.

Sewage from many towns and cities ends up in the sea. Sometimes it has not been fully treated and carries diseases like typhoid. People risk falling ill if they swim near sewage outfalls or eat shellfish from nearby. Bacteria normally break the sewage down, using oxygen from the water. In shallow, sheltered bays there is sometimes not enough sea water to dilute the sewage. The bacteria may use up so much oxygen that there is not enough left for the fish and they may die.

Fertilisers used by farmers are washed into the sea. Plant plankton can now grow very fast because of the extra nitrates. Fish may not be able to live in the new conditions, and swim away or die.

In recent years, oil pollution from damaged oil tankers or rigs has affected many waters. Oil kills seaweeds, shellfish and plankton. This can disrupt food chains, leaving many animals with no food. The oil clogs the feathers of the seabirds. They cannot fly, so they starve. When they preen, they swallow oil which is very harmful. Many birds are killed by oil spillages.

We discharge hundreds of different factory chemicals into the sea. Sometimes more harmful chemicals get there by accident, including pesticides and radioactive wastes from nuclear power stations. Some of these chemicals are poisonous – mercury, lead and DDT are examples. Unlike sewage which is broken down, many of them stay in the sea for a long time.

If poisonous substances are concentrated they may kill at once. Diluted by sea water, small quantities may be absorbed into plankton without killing them. Animals feeding on the plankton take in the poison. The poison stays in their bodies, and as they eat more it builds up. Eventually, animals like sharks, sea birds and man at the top of the food chain may become poisoned.

The sea is also a rubbish tip for plastic items. These do not rot like paper. Some sea creatures get tangled up in discarded fishing line and nets, and die. Some swallow plastic items thinking they are food.

Coastal waters are most affected by pollution. However, the large oceans and their creatures are also at risk. Pollutants can be transported long distances by winds, currents, and in the food chains. DDT has even been found in penguins in the Antarctic, thousands of miles away from where it was used by man.

In order to look after the sea and its inhabitants, we must control pollution. We must find more ways to dispose of our rubbish, and recycle more than we do now. We must also avoid accidental pollution of the sea.

Conservation of sea creatures

Mankind has had a big effect on many kinds of sea creatures. We have fished, collected or hunted some, often seriously reducing their numbers. We have poisoned others or destroyed their food supplies by polluting the seas. Yet we are still very dependent on sea creatures as a source of food and other materials. It is vital for our own survival that we conserve the sea and its creatures in the future.

World population is increasing. In the 1960s it reached three billion. Before the year 2000 it is expected to reach six billion. All these additional people will need food. We already get a lot of food from the sea, but we could probably get more. It is important that we conserve the populations we harvest through sustained use, so that we can go on using them for many years. However, we will probably develop more farming of sea animals in the future. Farming is very productive and will help to feed some of the extra people.

International commissions have been set up to watch over some of the sea animals being fished or hunted. They often decide on the maximum amount of animals which can be taken without damaging the populations. The Northeast Atlantic Fisheries Commission controls the amount of fish each country can catch in the North Sea. The International Whaling Commission banned the hunting of those whale species which were in serious danger of extinction.

Unfortunately, some sea creatures are already extinct. Many others are threatened with extinction now. The cause is often man's activities. Threatened species are listed in Red Data Books which draw attention to their plight. The books outline each species's situation, how many are left and what needs to be done to conserve them. These books are produced by the International Union for Conservation of Nature which works to protect animals and plants. A closely related organisation is the The World Wide Fund for Nature (World Wildlife Fund).

In many parts of the world, people are now much more aware of the problems of over-using animal populations and of pollution. Some action is being taken, but much more needs to be done. In many cases co-operation between different countries is needed. This is vital, or we risk losing some very valuable resources. Populations take a long time to build up again. Some never recover. Once a species is extinct, it is gone forever.

Key
1 monk seal
2 fur seal
3 bowhead whale
4 blue whale
5 green turtle
6 Galapagos penguin
7 flightless cormorant
8 Pacific Ridley turtle
9 sea otter

Index

This map of the world shows the differences in ocean depths. The palest blue areas show quite shallow water, while the darker blue areas indicate very deep water.

0m–200m

200m–1000m

1000m–4000m

4000m–11,000m